Their Whispers
Tell A Story

Memoirs of a
Psychic/Medium

Janny Di

authorHOUSE®

AuthorHouse™
1663 Liberty Drive
Bloomington, IN 47403
www.authorhouse.com
Phone: 1-800-839-8640

Published by AuthorHouse 3/13/2013

ISBN: 978-1-4817-2295-7 (sc)
ISBN: 978-1-4817-2294-0 (hc)
ISBN: 978-1-4817-2293-3 (e)

Library of Congress Control Number: 2013904022

Introduction

"Our bodies die but our energy remains."

I'd like to introduce myself. My real name is Janice DiMaggio Pietzak. I go by the name of Janny Di. Janny is a nickname that was lovingly given to me by a good friend of mine many years ago and I always loved it. DI is in honor of my family name which all of us DiMaggio's are really proud of. I became aware of my gifts at a very early age but I never imagined I would be able to use them in such a positive way. When I think of the crazy rollercoaster I've been on in this lifetime I kind of understand why every event occurred the way it did. Life is an accumulation of lessons and if you are wise you learn from them.

I always knew I was "different" from others yet I never struggled with it. I have always been comfortable with my gifts. It was always second nature to me. I remember communicating with my Mom almost telepathically before she passed. A sense or awareness of events that were about to unfold that both of us were prepared for. Many people may think of this as odd, I always thought of it as normal.

Sicilian on my father's side and Yugoslavian on my mother's, I follow tradition from both sides of my heritage and am honored to be called "Strega","Vjestica" or Witch. I do practice the "craft" and hope that someday people will stop fearing and educate themselves on what the craft truly is about. Some of the most caring, just, intelligent people I know are witches. I am proud to be associated with them. If everyone respected other's religions and beliefs the world would be an amazing place. Just like one of my idols John Lennon sang…..Imagine…..

"*Their Whispers Tell A Story, Memoirs of a Psychic/Medium*" is a combination of some of the events that have taken place in my lifetime. It also documents some of my beliefs on different topics and hopefully opens some doors of spirituality and understanding for each and every one who reads it.

Enjoy and Blessings to you all . . . . .Janny

I don't wear a cape for attention. Nor do I try to intimidate others with my so-called power. I live my life with integrity, humor, honesty, generosity and grace. I listen, advise, have patience and rise above. I know where I come from and honor my ancestors, the elderly and tradition. I respect others, protect the innocent, care for animals and take pride in my home, family and self. I do not succumb to pettiness or jealousy. I know my self-worth and do not waste my time casting against anyone who is on an "Ego Trip" because they are powerless. I recognize the signs, respect the Earth, call to the winds and understand I am but a thread in this vast tapestry called the Universe. I do not like having enemies but will never tolerate false accusations, gossip and downright cruelty. Never mistake my kindness for weakness and understand I am what I am from the depths of my soul. I respect my "Craft" and take pride and pleasure in honing my skills. We are unique, proud and timeless. We are WITCHES!
Janny Di

Dedication

To my children Jesse and Kali my greatest accomplishments, I adore you. Thanks to my husband Harold for all his love and support as well as the rest of my amazing family. Thank you Mom and guides for always being there.

Also Christian Day for taking a chance on me, Leeanne Marrama for the encouragement, Lori "mama" Bruno for reminding me to reach for the stars and to always be true to myself.

Last but not least love to Andrew Mitchell and my soul sister Kelly Curtis Spangler for all your guidance in helping my dreams come true!

To My Salem Family.....YOU ROCK!

Contents

Part Two – "The Family Connection"

Part Three – "On To the Next Generation"

Part Four – "Animals and Demons"

Part Five – "And In the End......."

Part One

"Everything Happens for a Reason"

Chapter One

"Changes"

We were all so happy to have Mom home again. She had recently been released from the hospital. Walking Pneumonia is not something you can mess around with. We were lucky the doctors caught it in time and assumed we were home free. I remember the adults commenting on how she needed to slow down and rest. The one thing I knew about my mom was she was like a bull and she never sat still. Grandma Di stayed with us the month she was away. We loved our grandma but there's no one like Mom.

It was a usual Sunday morning. The birds were singing and spring was in the air. Little did any of us know how our worlds would be turned upside down that day. Dad was at the stove making pancakes and my sister Dee was sitting at the kitchen table. I adored Sundays. We got to eat pancakes and Daddy was home all day. My dad was a great man not only to his children but to anyone who ever had the pleasure of making his acquaintance.

My job that morning was to wake up my mom. I ran into the bedroom and jumped into the bed. I remember seeing all the clothing trunks in the room halfway filled in anticipation of our trip to Italy. My mom was so excited to finally go home so she could show her parents her precious little girls. It had been 15 years since she had been home. During that time she married and had two children, Denise age 9 (my sister) and Janice age 6.

"Mommy, Mommy, get up! Maaaaaa GET UP!" No response. I put my hands on her face and kissed her cheek. She felt a little cold. Once more I yelled, "Mommy!" There was still no response. I jumped out of the bed and ran into the kitchen. "Dad, Mommy won't get up. She won't stop sleeping." My father looked at me and said, "Go try again sweetie. She'll get up." "Okay, I'll try again." Off I ran down the hall back into the bedroom. I jumped into the bed once more and whispered in her ear. "Mommy, please get up." I leaned back and was very surprised to feel the bed was wet. I darted back into the kitchen while saying," Daddy, Mom still won't wake up and she made pee pee in the bed. "I remember a brief look of confusion on my father's face. Then within seconds he dropped the spatula in the pan and ran into the bedroom. My sister and I both followed in after him. We stood in the doorway as we saw our father break down. "Marisa, please Marie, my Marie. "He held her head in his arms and turned to us. With tear filled eyes he said," Girls, go to your room." I looked at him and asked, " Daddy, what's wrong?" "GO TO YOUR ROOM!" He raised his voice and we listened. Daddy never yelled. My sister and I looked at each other and we quickly scrambled across the hall to our room.

We sat together on my sister's bed that morning watching a barrage of firemen and police enter our small apartment. We finally saw a familiar face. Grandma Di was here. She grabbed the both of us in her arms and just wept. That was the turning point for me. I now went from total confusion to pure terror. "What's wrong with Mommy?" I asked with no response. "WHAT'S WRONG WITH MOMMY?" I could not control my shouting or my tears. I didn't want my mom to go away again.

At that point my dad had come in because of the yelling. He looked at us with tears in his eyes and spoke the hardest words he would ever have to say to us. "Mommy's gone girls. She's in heaven now. I know this is hard but you have to try to be brave. Your mother wouldn't want you to cry.

"Gone? Mommy's gone? I don't want Mommy to be gone. Who is going to take care of us now?" I proceeded to cry a river of tears. I looked up at my older sister and noticed she just sat there quietly her eyes watering. "Dee Dee? How come you aren't crying? "She looked at me holding back her own tears and said, "Because if you really love Mommy you won't cry. She wouldn't want us to cry." To this day my sister never ceases to amaze me on how well she can control her emotions. I wish I had half the emotional strength she does. My father was back down the short hallway standing there expressionless while they wheeled my mother out on the gurney. He followed them out a broken man.

That night I dreamt of my mother. I remembered how safe I felt in her arms. I remembered how she spoke to me with her eyes when we got in that car accident and I slammed my head. I remembered how she told me I was going to be okay with her mind when I had pneumonia. I thought it was normal to communicate without speaking. Every child is attached to their parent and it never dawned on me that any of this communication was extraordinary or unique, yet it was. It was the beginning of the psychic link.

Chapter Two

"The Awakening"

Everything was going so quickly. I would not leave my big sister's side. Grandma Di was staying with us again and I still wasn't really clear on what was going on. We were bathed, dressed and ready to go. Off to the viewing. To this day I don't really know why we were taken to the wake but in retrospect it had to be. Everything in life happens for a reason and I needed to be there to understand exactly what my "gift" was. I know if my mother would have lived longer (she never expected to pass at thirty -four) she would have helped me come into my own. After all, she was the one who passed her abilities on to me. She started me off at such an early age, communicating with me almost telepathically. As I stated previously, I never thought it was anything out of the norm.

There were so many people crying and carrying on. All the ogling at us by total strangers while they shook their heads. It was such an odd day. I was tired and bored and wanted to go home. We had stopped at the store earlier and I won a ring out of the gumball machine. Six years old and bored out of my mind, I tossed the ring and was rolling the plastic bubble it came in across the floor. Up and down the aisles I crawled flicking the case with my finger. Just as I rounded the next row of chairs I heard a voice. It was soft and sweet and so familiar. It was my mom. "Now why is my baby girl crawling on her knees in such a beautiful dress?" "Mom?" I looked up and to my surprise there she stood smiling away. My beautiful mommy was leaning against her coffin watching me crawl through the chairs. She was glowing like an angel.

I had many imaginary friends as I was growing up. All ages, male and female but never knew any of them. Now here I was at my mother's wake seeing double. One mommy asleep in the coffin and the other one standing there smiling at me. "Mom?" I blurted. "Shhhhhhhh , not so loud sweetie. It's me." She whispered back. "Mommy, everyone says you are with God? Where did you go? Why did you leave us? We all need you!" She responded "Sweetie, listen to mommy. I didn't chose to leave yet but I had no choice. Mommy is in a wonderful place right now It's even more special because I get to watch you and your sister anytime I want. I will never ever leave you. I will be with you all the time and others who are 'special' like you and I will see me too! Remember how we play our game of talking without using our lips? Well nothing has changed. I will be with you always guiding you and I will help you to understand," "Mommy, I want to play with you and do things with you and hug you." I responded. She replied," I love you my girl. Things have changed now. When you fall asleep and dream, I will be there and we can play and draw and do all those things we love to do together. I promise you that."

"Honey, who are you talking to?" My father was looking at me with worry and concern on his face. "It's Mommy, she's standing right there Dad." I pointed to the coffin and looked up at him. My dad hugged me and said, "Oh sweetie, I can't imagine what you are feeling right now but Mommy is with God."" I know Dad but she says she is here with us too and she always will be!" My father turned towards the coffin with tears in his eyes. He just smiled at me and said," Okay sweetheart, if you say so." He walked away slowly rubbing his forehead. His expression was one of confusion and concern. He thought I was so overwhelmed with grief that I was hallucinating, when in reality I was communicating. I don't really remember much more about the wake or the funeral after that. I think it was partly because I was so confused about what was going on and partly because I knew in my heart that she wasn't really gone. I know her body was in that box and I know that I saw that box being lowered into the ground, yet I had to believe that I would see her again. Little did I know that this was just the beginning.

Chapter Three
"A New Home"

Everything was changing so quickly. Mommy was gone (well so everyone said) and we were moving out of our apartment. I always had a wonderful childhood. Our apartment building had a huge backyard with lots of green grass, a teeter totter and a swing set. A little farther down was a picnic table with a trellis and fig trees winding through the wood. We had spent many a summer day at that table playing with clay and letting our imaginations run free.

It was a great place to live. There was always someone around to play with. If we weren't outside we were down the hall at the elderly couples 'place talking to their birds. They had 2 parrots that loved children and we spent many hours there feeding them bread and a bit of red wine. It was going to be hard to leave all that behind especially our friends.

We were only moving across the city. We had been to Grandma Di's house plenty of times. It was nice enough but it was grandma's house. It was a new house, new school, new rules. I remember how odd grandma's house felt even though we had been there so many times before. At first my sister and I slept on a pull out couch in the den. It was different than having your own room. Eventually my father added an extension onto the back of the house that became our bedroom.

Adjusting to all the new things in our lives thankfully came easy. We formed new friendships at school and the teachers were very understanding. The only thing I ever had an issue with was the whispers. There went the poor girls that lost their mom. I got so tired of people telling me they were sorry that she was gone. She was no longer here but my bond was stronger than ever. She came to me frequently. I always knew she was around because I always sensed her or heard her whisper in my ear. She greeted me in the morning and was the last person I saw before I went to sleep at night.

Life was moving on. During those young years I started to take an interest in the paranormal and anything to do with the unexplained. I often kept things to myself because every time I mentioned my mother to my dad I could see the sadness in his eyes. He loved her so deeply that I do believe the pain never left him.

Grandma Di believed in one thing and one thing only. That was to be a devout Catholic. Her beliefs never went past the thought of having a God, Jesus Christ. There was no talk of afterlife, reincarnation or any such nonsense in our house. I remember her commenting on a woman who always used to talk about seeing apparitions. She was "pazzo".* You were born, you died, you were judged, went to Heaven or Hell and that was it, end of story.

---

* pazzo—crazy, mad, insane, lunatic in the Italian language.

Chapter Four
"Here We Go Again"

We were all settled into Grandma Di's house and life was getting back to normal. I remember all those nights I cried for my mother because even though I could see her, I couldn't feel her wrap her arms around me. Sometimes I think that's why she is always by my side all these years later. I feel like she wants to make it up to me. We cannot control our death so I really don't feel that way but I have to admit I'm very selfish about having her around. I was now approaching nine and once again felt that feeling of security in my life. My older sister was going on twelve and was nice and content. That's when the winds of change began to blow.

Dad had met someone. He was dating her for a while and things had gotten serious. Her name was Annette. As time went by, things progressed and they were married. My dad renovated grandma's place to make a separate apartment for us. Within three years my dad found a house he purchased and we were moving out.

Yonkers was about fifteen minutes away from grandmas. I think the transition for us wasn't so devastating because quite honestly we moved onto another block filled with kids of every age. There was always something to do. I missed my friends from

New Rochelle and would visit often. After a while like everything else people move on. You form new friendships and so do your old friends. Everyone remained friendly although we just didn't see each other as often.

Chapter Five

"Anthony"

On September 28th, 1970 my brother was born. I remember the day he came home from the hospital. Annette (my stepmother) got out of the car with a little yellow bundle in her arms.

My father was thrilled he finally had a son! It was nice to have a little brother. My sister and I were quite a bit older and this was great for us. We had a new little baby in the house. He was absolutely adorable. The three of us bonded immediately and remain very close to this day.

Anthony was such a great kid. He was always very creative and you never knew what surprises you would find when he was around. I remember once he took all the green plastic containers the strawberries came in and built a water tower in the bath tub.

Life was wonderful. My dad renovated the whole house and it was absolutely beautiful. My sister and I both baby sat for Anthony and time was flying by. The years were passing by happily and Anthony was turning 3. Once again life dealt us a tragic hand. It was the beginning of another long hard road we were forced to go down.

Chapter Six

"Accidents Happen.........Again?"

I remember the phone call coming in. I was in New Rochelle visiting my friends and was told dad had an accident. They said that he was okay and I remember not even wanting to go home. What I thought was a little accident was actually a near fatal one. When I got to Yonkers I was told the truth. My father was putting a new roof on the garage. He somehow slipped and while his body landed in the grass, his head hit the concrete sidewalk. A large part of his skull had shattered and he was in bad shape. Head injuries are hard to judge. The swelling had to go down before they could see what was happening.

After I was told what was going on I ran upstairs to my bedroom and threw myself on the bed. I remember saying over and over "Please don't take my dad from me!" I don't know how long I was crying but I was exhausted and distraught. Suddenly I saw a small ball of light forming in the corner of my room near the door.

Chapter Seven

"The Messenger"

I looked at the light with amazement. The ball was growing larger and larger. The illumination coming from it was incredible. It started to stretch and elongate. Before I knew it the ball had taken a shape of a human close to what looked to be about 7 feet tall. As I watched astonished it continued to take shape and grow. Eventually it revealed what it was. There before me stood an angel. I could not tell you if it was male or female. It spoke in such a harmonious tone. It felt like time stood still.

I was amazed at this beautiful vision. The Angel spoke to me and said," Dry your tears your father is fine. It is not his time to leave this place yet. "Suddenly an unbelievable feeling of peace came over me and I actually began to smile. I knew in my soul that he would be okay. Within a split second of delivering the message the angel was gone. I wiped my tears and walked down the steps.

My grandma and other family members were sitting on the couch filled with grief. When I reached the bottom step I said boldly," He's going to be fine! "Everyone looked at me and with sympathy in their eyes. I repeated," He's going to be fine!" Now I don't know how long after I proclaimed that statement that we got the phone call but we did and dad was showing signs of improvement. He pulled through the emergency surgery and was in ICU. He was stable and being moved again, this time into a regular room.

Now I know for a fact that was an angel I saw in my room. I haven't seen him since yet I know he/she is there. That was one of the most incredible experiences in my life. To be present in the light that strongly is something you never forget. I do feel that was my guardian angel that came to me that early evening to comfort me and deliver the message. I often feel him around me along with the support from many others.

Dad was doing well. He was recovering from his injuries and was told he would need to have a metal plate put into his head. The surgeon wanted to wait a year or so before he performed the surgery. It would freak me out when I would think of there being a "soft spot" in his skull. He would often joke about it and say, "I need that like I need this hole in my head!" Corny yes but I would give a million dollars to hear him say that again. Eventually he did go back into the hospital have the surgery. I believe that was the same year I turned fourteen.

Chapter Eight

"Life Can Be So Unfair"

It was November 16th and for the first time in a long time my step mother Annette was in the Christmas spirit. She actually had the Christmas tree up redecorating it to get it just right for the holiday.

My father had since enclosed the back porch and it was now our brand new family room. Winter was on the way and he wanted to put heat in the extension before it got too cold. I remember I was in the basement listening to music.

Being a typical teenager my music at was blasting. Suddenly I thought I heard screaming. I lowered the volume and realized that it was Annette screaming from the top of the basement stairs. She was yelling, "Something happened to your father!"

I darted up the stairs unprepared for what I was going to find. There lying on the floor in front of the kitchen sink was my father. He had just finished installing the new heating system in the family room and was washing his hands. He had a massive heart attack.

Everything was kind of blurry after that. I remember my sister Dee coming in and telling her to call the ambulance. I also remember attempting to give him mouth to mouth but honestly was not trained and had no clue what I was doing.

It was too late. He was gone. Once again I was there. Eight years after finding my mom I was watching my father's spirit leave. It is just another painful memory that remains forever. Until this day when I hear the song that was on that night I turn it off. My father doesn't come to me often but when he does it's for a reason. It's usually when I am going through a tough time in my life.

The wake and the funeral went by. You just kind of go through the motions. This time at age fourteen I understood what death was. This time it was different. I didn't see my father standing by his coffin. I didn't feel him around me at all. When the time came to say goodbye, I kissed him on his forehead and remember how cold his skin was against my lips. It was final. He was gone. A part of me was buried with my father that day.

Chapter Nine
"Reasons"

S o much has happened in my life and I believe every event leads you to exactly where you need to be. The following are just a few events that have occurred over the course of my lifetime. Some Life changing others just what they are. Either way, they are all signs and all happened for a reason.

My Dad used to say the same thing. He would say the reasons are not always apparent at first but in the long run you will see why. He was devastated when my mother died but if she didn't pass away he would have never met Annette and my wonderful brother Anthony and his beautiful family would not be here!

Everything is a series of events. My father's death caused me to eventually live with my grandmother again. I would have never moved back to New Rochelle but if I didn't I would have probably never met my husband. We are now married for twenty-six years and despite our ups and downs are still together. Out of our union have come two of the most amazing people I know, my son Jesse and my daughter Kali. I really do believe that the two of them are on this Earth for a purpose. They would not be who they are with anyone else but Harold as their father and me as their mom. Besides them making me feel like the luckiest woman alive, they will both make their mark someday. If you live long enough life cycles around and I don't plan on going anywhere for a very long time.

Chapter Ten

"Jeanine"

About ten years ago I met a wonderful woman named Jeanine. One of those people that you know just made the world a better place. Funny, kind, sweet, willing to help anyone at any time. Our children went to the same school and we grew to be friends. She was always collecting gifts or money for children who didn't have anything around the holidays and always volunteered for events when she was needed. I really was fond of her and was blessed to have her in my life.

After our children graduated, we lost touch. I would hear about her occasionally. She was working at an elementary school as an aide. At that time I was working at a toy store as a cashier. One May afternoon she came in with a child to use the restroom. I was so happy to see her. I remember thinking she looked a bit tired and her face seemed a bit swollen.

She just didn't look quite right. We started to chat a bit and she told me she was experiencing pain in her back for a while now. She always had digestive problems when she was younger but I didn't know how serious it was. She explained that she was going to have surgery to remove her gall bladder. She was scheduled for the operation in a few weeks. I wished her well hugged her and told her we would get together over the summer.

Although she didn't look right to me I never expected to receive the news I did.

A few weeks later she had the surgery. When they operated they found the pain she was experiencing was due to cancer. It was already in an advanced stage and the only thing they could do was make her comfortable.

My friend died quickly. She was only forty-five. She left behind her husband and daughter whom she adored. Her death truly devastated me.

The funeral was very sad. When someone that young goes no one really gets it. Her cousin a Deacon spoke at the church. One of the things he said was "When I saw my cousin in the hospital, she had come to terms with her passing. She accepted her death." Wow. All I could think was how can you accept your death when you had your whole life ahead of you? Is this what she chose? Did she choose to leave her daughter behind? Sometimes I think I just over analyze things and I should let it be.

Her life on this plane was definitely way too short. I was so sad to have lost my friend and her death affected me more than I could ever imagine. I often thank Jeanine for making me change my outlook about life. No more wasting time thinking about things I wanted to do. She is one of the reasons why I got up and did them.

Chapter Eleven

"Karma and Living Clean"

I have personally had struggles with my own children. When I have questioned "why" at times one of the answers I got, "That's their Karma. It's not your problem. "Um ,this is my child, one of the most important people in my life.IT IS MY PROBLEM! So, if it is what I have chosen and I need to learn something, why does he/she have to suffer? If it is their Karma and they need to learn something, why does the rest of the family have to suffer? Sorry but something just doesn't sit right with me.

I fully support living your life "clean." By that I mean being the best "You" that you can be. People should help each other and be kind to each other. On the other side of the coin, not everyone lives that way.

I was speaking to someone at a workshop I took and what she said made a lot of sense. The workshop was about finding your inner light and connecting. There were over 100 people all feeling healed , connected and happy. You could tell by her body language this poor woman was a ball of nerves and anxiety. I went over to her and tried to tell her to just let stuff go before it killed her. In the bigger scheme of things is this issue really that important? What she replied made a lot of sense. She said," That's all fine and well while we are here but what happens when we go back to the real world? People can be really cruel and don't take the time to be kind."

I looked at her and thought she was absolutely right. The whole theory of living your life in the light is a very difficult thing to do when not everyone around you does. I have heard of some shady people who are the first ones to attend mass Easter morning after murdering someone the night before. The whole theory of everyone living in peace and harmony is a lovely thought but will never be a reality. Not as long as humans have emotions. Jealousy, competition, anger, as long as these exist, living your life "clean" will always be a challenge.

The other problem is where does the line begin and where does it end? What I mean by that is do you continually have to be a doormat? I know I can be patient and kind and so may you but what about the other billions of people on the face of the Earth?

It is very hard to take the higher road when dealing with immaturity and jealousy. This brings me back to Karma. In order for my "Karma" to be okay do I have to take everyone's crap? No and I won't. However what I will do is try my best to be positive and when I run into negativity, I will wish that person well and get them OUT OF MY LIFE ! Negativity breeds negativity.. Get rid of it! Like my mentor Lori Bruno always says " CLEAN HOUSE!".

"The world is a circle. ""What comes around goes around." These are all very common sayings that stem from the concept of Karma. The definition of Karma is as follows: Destiny or fate following as effect from cause. In other words, every action you take whether good or bad will result in a reaction from the Universe.

Being human we all get caught up in "Things." It makes us feel good to have the newest phone, a designer item or a new hairstyle. Unfortunately all these "Things" generate envy and competition. Instead of "One-upping" each other, we should be trying to help each other. If you ever think about all the excess we live with it is crazy.

There are little things a person can do to help their Karma and there are big things you can do. Either way if your heart is in the right place things will always pan out. Following are what I consider the big Karmic No-Nos.

* DON'T EVER PLAY WITH SOMEONE'S HEART. This is one of the worst things you can ever do. When someone opens their heart to you and lays it on the line , that means they have trusted you enough to tell you their deepest darkest secrets and their emotional being is in your hands. This is a great responsibility and it is not to be taken lightly.

Being a card reader and advisor I often council people with their problems. One must be very careful as to what they say because a single word can change a person's life. Not always for the better. Don't ever lead someone on, blow them off, or betray them. It is better to be open, honest and up front. You may hurt someone's feelings but in the long run you are better off. Honesty is always the best policy.

* DON'T EVER SPEAK ILL OF ANOTHER PERSON'S CHILD OR CHILDREN. If a child's actions are not what you expect remember they are usually a product of who is raising them. This is not always the case but the majority of the time it is. Children like animals are innocent. Hurting either one of them is just a major no no. So the next time you hear someone gossiping about another one's child, remind them that their little precious one still has to grow up too!

* DON'T EVER MESS WITH SOMEONE'S LIVELIHOOD. It is tough enough in this economy to keep a job. If you mess with someone's income maliciously there will be a grave price to pay. It may come as a job loss or lack of funds. All I know is you can bet your life it will come around.

* NEVER EVER HURT THE INNOCENT. This means animals, children, the elderly. Anyone who tortures animals for fun is a sick individual.

It also means they are showing psychopathic behavior so stay clear. Child abusers need to be beat themselves and so does anyone who abuses the elderly. If someone doesn't have the patience to care for a child they should not have any. If they don't have the patience to care for a child or an elderly person they should change their occupation. Leave those jobs for people who are capable of caring for them.

* YOU ABSOLUTELY CANNOT GO AROUND LIFE INTENTIONALLY HURTING ANYONE! As you can see I'm pretty adamant about that one. Some people are so unhappy in their own lives they feel the need to go around hurting others. Not a good thing to do! If you do run into someone like that it usually means they are so unhappy in their own life they want to drag you down with them. Misery loves company.

Chapter Twelve

"Dreams"

Experts all have a different opinion about what dreams are all about. Some have a scientific explanation for everything. Scientific or not, there are just some dreams that cannot be explained. Just like there are occurrences that cannot be explained.

Some experts say dreams are nothing but fears or anxieties. Others say wishes etc. Most likely a majority of our dreams have an explanation. It can consist of movies we've seen or subjects we've discussed. What about those dreams that you know have a message? The one that wakes you up in the middle of the night with a sense of urgency or are the first thing you think of when you awaken.

I do believe that when our bodies and minds are at rest, a doorway opens to receive things we normally can't. When we are awake there is too much stimulation around us. I do know that there are different kinds of dreams too. Reoccurring dreams , premonitions and messages from the dead. One of the first things I tell people to do is leave a pen and pad near their bed. When you do have a dream in the middle of the night that wakes you up out of your sleep, WRITE IT DOWN! You will be amazed at how things start to make sense as the day goes on. It is always nice to have a reference.

Chapter Thirteen
"Reoccurring Dreams"

When someone has a reoccurring dream it can mean a few different things. In my own personal experience I feel it is a case of remembering a past life or reincarnation. When we reincarnate we are not supposed to bring our memories into the next life. Just like other unexplained things in life sometimes we do. When we dream, we remember. Following are examples of different kinds of dreams.

"The Lady In Blue"

I am walking on a wooden boardwalk. I can see and hear the water beneath me. It is a beautiful day and I am holding a parasol. The parasol is light blue with white lace around it. I am wearing a long light blue dress that looks to be from the Victorian Era. I am wearing white gloves and am enjoying the sound my button up boots are making on the wood.

The sky is blue, it is warm and I can feel the slight breeze blowing in my face. I am strolling slowly with a feeling of contentment and happiness. I know that I come from a family of wealth and prestige.

My hair is pinned up with a small blue satin hat sitting on my head tilted to one side. Even though I don't look like myself, I know that it is me. There's recognition in the eyes. After all the eyes are the doorway to the soul. No one is near me, nothing is happening. I am just strolling contently down the boardwalk. I can even smell the ocean beneath me. I take deep breaths and continue walking. I have had the dream over six times and it's always the same. Okay so that's the big dream. Like I said there is nothing happening but I have to pay attention to the things that are prominent.

* The Victorian Era

* The color light blue

* The Sea

*Walking

*My boots

After having this particular dream so many times I have tried to analyze what it is all about. These are the things I have come up with thus far. As far as the Victorian Era goes, I seem to have a little obsession with that particular time period. I adore the clothing, hats, houses and more. When I went to San Francisco for the first time, I had a connection to it that I just couldn't explain. I felt like I had been there before. The other places I always feel a real connection to is Cape May, New Jersey and of course Salem, Massachusetts.

Now if you think about it things kind of make sense. I know instinctively that I am from a very prominent family. I believe we may have traveled across the country and either resettled in the east or had a business that covered both coasts.

Cape May is a beautiful quaint little area that has little brightly painted houses and amazing Victorian architecture. Originally settled during the colonial era, there was a great fire in 1878. When it was rebuilt a surge of Victorian styled buildings were created. I must have been there in a past life which would explain my present day love of all things Victorian.

I absolutely love the seaside. It's one of the places that I truly feel at peace. I also am an avid walker. I love to just throw on my sneakers and go. I also feel that the fact that I am in constant motion may be an indication of what is going on in my life. I am constantly striving to move forward. From what I have read on what boots in a dream mean, it represents strength. Not physical strength but an inner strength about something you feel strongly about. Taking a stand on something.

The only piece of this puzzle I have yet to figure out is all the light blue satin. I like the color light blue but it isn't particularly a favorite. I have read that it represents creativity. It is also the color associated with peace and the Blessed Mother. Perhaps it is a sign of my faith.

Chapter Fourteen

"Premonitions"

Premonitions can come to anyone at any time. It's just a matter of figuring out what the reason is. Most of the premonitions I have had are for other people and they are never really on a grand scale. By this I mean I am not one to predict earthquakes and tsunamis but I am really good with names and unfortunately death.

One of the clearest premonitions I had was of a pregnancy. I had a dream that my girlfriend's grandfather came to me. He was chatting away and mentioned he died of colon cancer. Then he said that my girlfriend was going to have another baby and it was finally going to be a boy. At that time she had two girls a few years apart from each other and had no intention of going for a third. Her youngest was about nine.

A few days later I saw her after school when we were waiting for the kids. I started to tell her about my dream. The minute I mentioned her grandfather and colon cancer her eyes grew wide. She had told me that he had died of colon cancer years previously. Then when I delivered the message about the pregnancy, she looked at me and said, "Well, you were right about my grandfather but at the moment I am not even thinking about having another baby!" We laughed it off and let it be.

The next September when the kids were back to school, I saw her walking towards me. She had recently found out she was pregnant! The following April she had her son. It is really funny how there are certain people you run into in your lifetime that you feel a total connection to. My friend Wendy is one of them. Every time I get a feeling or dream something about her it comes to pass. I really feel that we were somehow connected in a past life.

Fifteen

"Dreaming of the Dead"

Now dreaming of the dead is a subject that fascinates me. Everyone who has had a dream of those who have passed has a different take on what exactly the dream means. Sometimes there are warnings in the messages, other times just news of things to come.

My neighbor Anthony lost his mom a few years ago. She was such a sweet woman and was taken way before her time. Anthony was very close to his mom and always loves to hear from her.

He told me that he got a call from his cousin out of the clear blue sky. His cousin said she had a dream that she saw his mom holding a baby boy. She wasn't saying anything she just stood there. Anthony proceeded to tell his cousin the news. His girlfriend was pregnant and they just found out it was a boy!

Was it a message from the dead or coincidence? Who knows? As I stated previously everyone has a different take on it. In my experience every dream I have had of the dead had some message behind it. I also noticed that whenever I do dream of the dead there is one thread in common. When I have tried to touch or hug someone who has passed I get the same reaction. They step back or put their hands up and tell me "No." I have wondered why this is the case and the conclusion I have come to is as follows. I think I am not to touch them because I am on a different vibration then they are and it will break the connection. There is a doorway that opens when we sleep and if we try to connect by touching those who have gone through this doorway might close.

I have had many dreams of those who have passed around a birthday or an anniversary. Quite often the dreams I have aren't even for me. They are for someone I know who needs the message. I have read that when a person has psychic ability the dead recognize that and a light shines a bit brighter to them. When a light is there the dead are drawn to that person because they know the chances of being heard are greater. Mediums become the voice for the dead. Here is an example of one of the dreams I had about 17 years ago.

Chapter Sixteen
"Message for My Daughter"

This was definitely one of those dreams that had a distinct message in it. It was about my mother in law. My mother in law Nicky was a wonderful woman who had a very close relationship with her daughter, my sister in law Joann. When "Mom" passed away unexpectedly as you can imagine the entire family was devastated. I think Jo took it hardest. She was the only daughter and moved back into the house after her divorce. Mom passed away quickly on February 17th 1991.

About four years later, I dreamt of mom. She looked absolutely radiant. In my dream I was sitting in church alone in a pew. She walked over to me, sat down next to me and smiled. I remember saying to myself," How could this be? Mom is gone. How is she here?"

As if she heard my thoughts she said," I am here because I need you to talk to my daughter Joann." Mom proceeded to tell me that she was having a very hard time going where she needed to go. She needed to go into the light but Joann was not letting her do so. It wasn't that she was doing this intentionally but because of Jo's overwhelming grief she wasn't allowing her to be free to move into the light.

When mom was done speaking, she smiled at me and walked away. The dream was so vivid and so real as soon as I awoke I called

Joann. As I was explaining what her mother said, she started to cry. I apologized for upsetting her and she said it wasn't me. She had just put a memorial into the newspaper that week for her mother. She told me that it was a particularly hard time for her at the moment and mom had been on her mind more than usual. I delivered the whole message and explained to her that she needs to start living her life and being happy. That is what mom wanted for her.

Now, think what you will but after that event it seemed that Joann came more to terms with her mother's death. Of course we always remember and with memories there's sadness. I think when we hear from the dead it puts our minds at ease a bit more. It is very comforting.

I have dealt with many people who want to hear from their loved ones. It's funny how that works. When I have someone come to me for messages the first thing I explain is who you want to come through and who comes through can be two very different things. In life if someone really doesn't have anything to say to you, normally you won't hear from them. Well it's the same way in death. You would never pick up the phone to call someone if you had nothing to say. I know this can be disappointing but that's just the way it goes.

Seventeen

"Is There A Reason Why I See Them Before They Die?"

Now I have run that question through my mind repeatedly. I have had three separate occasions I can think of where I saw someone and then found out shortly after that they had passed. One of the three was my friend Jeanine that I mentioned in a previous chapter. I knew in my heart something was wrong but it could have been so many things. I never imagined she would be so sick and not even know it.

One of the other people I saw before his death was a boy named Justin. I knew him from when he was a little boy. He was always one of the kindest, respectful, sweetest kids I have ever had the pleasure of knowing.

I was working near my home at the time. The establishment I was working at was one of a row of stores in a mini mall of sorts. I was outside and I saw Justin walking over to his car. Being the doll he was, the minute he saw me he came right over. He gave me a kiss and greeted me with a big smile on his face. We chatted for about five minutes or so. He asked about my children and my friend Val. Val and I ran a program in the school Justin attended when he was younger.

He told me he was working and I joked with him about the "real world" and how we realize we should never complain about being in school. I also asked for his mom and told him to hang in there and go to school. I went back to work with a smile on my face being so happy to know he was doing well.

A few days later I received a phone call from Val. She was sobbing into the phone and told me that Justin had been in a fatal car accident. I think he was only nineteen.

Do you ever get those moments in life when you just can't believe what you are hearing? It was taking some time for me to comprehend what she was saying. I think I said," But I just saw him a few days ago. "It's almost like the person couldn't be gone because you just saw them.

After I got off the phone, the thought crossed my mind about how he was the second person in a year I had seen before he passed. I have no idea what the reason for this is. In both cases I was at peace with myself knowing I saw both Jeanine and Justin and their beautiful smiling faces before they were taken from this place. Those beautiful memories will remain with me forever.

Chapter Eighteen
"The Mark of Death"

In both the previous instances I didn't really have a clue that either one of those two wonderful young people were going to pass. I can only recall one time when I felt death on its way. Unfortunately it was one of the most wonderful people I knew, my Uncle Jack.

Uncle Jack was one of those people that could always make you smile. He was my father's oldest brother and was so full of life it was amazing. He was a loyal son wonderful uncle, incredible husband and father. One of those guys that no one had a negative thing to say about.

For years my Uncle had parked his work truck in our yard. For years he would come every morning to have coffee with my Grandma Di before work. When the weather grew warm he would occasionally stop in for a beer before going home. After my grandma died, we still lived in the house and eventually bought it. Uncle Jack was still parking the truck in the yard.

It was June and the weather was getting really hot and unusually muggy. I was sitting on the front steps when he pulled in. I ran upstairs and grabbed a beer because it was stifling out. When he walked up front I gave him the beer and we chatted for a bit. He was standing on the steps with his elbow resting on the railing.

I remember just looking at his hand holding the beer and a feeling of dread came over me starting from the pit of my stomach. I just knew something bad was going to happen. I got a flash of what was about to unfold. It was alarmingly real. I know the expression on my face changed and he noticed. He even asked me if I was okay. I shook it off as well as I could and said I was fine. I prayed that night for my feeling to be wrong. As much as I prayed I could not get the thought out of my mind.

A few weeks passed and everyone was fine. The weather continued to grow hotter. I received a phone call from my cousin. It was not good news. Uncle Jack had fallen out of a window he was replacing. He was alive but in the hospital not doing well. I remember how my heart broke seeing him in the condition he was in. Seeing him there also brought back painful memories of my father's fall. Needless to say the outcome was not good.

Uncle Jack passed away. His funeral was one of the saddest and emotional funerals I have ever attended. More people got up to speak about him than you could ever imagine. It was a long beautiful funeral filled with tears.

That is the only time I can remember seeing death on someone I know and quite frankly, I hope never to see it again. When I do readings occasionally I have sensed the same presence on people. It is quite disturbing and needs to be handled delicately.

Chapter Nineteen

"Ending Up Where I Needed To Be"

It was August. I was out with a friend from High School. It was a time of big hair and kick ass metal. Back in the day there were a few local clubs we used to frequent often. I had just gotten out of a really bad 5 year relationship the previous March.

Ro and I were off and running once again at a local dive. There standing in the corner behind the sound board was my future husband. Now how did I know? I have no clue but I knew. It's so funny because when my father was alive he said a few profound things that have stuck with me all my life. This wasn't one of them but his words stuck with me nonetheless.

I would ask him," Dad, how will I know when I meet the man I should marry?" His answer," You'll just know." Well Dad, you were right again. I saw Harold and I knew. It was funny how I actually pointed him out to my friend Ro and said," That's my future husband." She replied, "Yeah Jan ,this week."

Well without getting into all the details about it, I did marry Harold and we are still together 26 years later. It has been a roller coaster ride but like I always say, "Whatever will be will be". Out of our union came two of the most amazing people I know, my son Jesse and my daughter Kali.

There's a funny thing about "knowing". I knew who I was going to marry, and I also knew I was carrying a boy with my first pregnancy and a girl with my second. Some like to call it "woman's Intuition". I call it "Knowing". Either way it's a gift I treasure.

Part Two

"The Family Connection"

Chapter Twenty

"It's In the Blood"

Over the years by speaking to people who have been sensitive to the unexplained, I have come to notice a pattern. Most people who are sensitive have siblings and other relatives that have the same abilities. Whether they choose to use it or not is a totally different story. In my family alone aside from my two children (who are both gifted) we have quite a few. All three of my nieces have had experiences. My nephew Dom (although he doesn't like to talk about it) and of course my sister. She is amazing!

I have a brother who also has a very strong "intuition" and I know his daughter Summer has it too. His other two children are still young although I have a hunch they may be gifted as well. Anthony and I have different mothers but my step mother Annette always sensed things. So does my sister in law Carolyn though she doesn't like to admit it. So actually we are a very intuitive family as a whole. It comes from different places but it is very prominent.

Chapter Twenty One

"Meant To Be"

Time was moving forward. Harold and I were renting the second floor apartment from Grandma Di. Life was good. We were married a little over two years when we decided to have a child. In July of 1989 Jesse was born. I knew from the minute I conceived that it was a boy. Jesse was meant to come into this world and I know someday he will do great things. Now, I know I sound like a typically proud Mom but there's more to the story. The moment I decided to have a child I conceived. It was amazingly quick.

When I was about 12 weeks into the pregnancy I had a little problem. I woke up in the middle of the night and went to the bathroom. When I got up I noticed I was bleeding. At first (because I was half asleep) I kind of just said to myself hmmm, it's that time of the month again. That's when the panic set in. I was pregnant. There should be no blood.

The next morning I spoke to the doctor. He was concerned. He also told me to stay put and don't do anything. He didn't even want me to come in. His wife (the assistant) got on the phone with me and was trying to explain that if I miscarry it usually means something was wrong with the baby. She was trying to comfort me and tell me there is no reason why I couldn't try again. I knew in my heart the baby was fine. Jesse came into this world posterior (face up). He didn't want to miss a thing and although it hasn't revealed itself yet his purpose will become known. He is incredibly intuitive. He is meant to be here.

Chapter Twenty Two

"Kissing My Grandson Goodbye"

When Jesse was born it was one of the happiest events my husband's family had in a long time. Things had changed quite a bit in the three years that I was married. My father -in-law had passed away unexpectedly from cancer. My Mother-in-law had a new found independence. She got her driver's license, had a new man in her life, lost a lot of weight and was doing fantastic. I don't mean to make her sound like she jumped into all this but she was in a very unhappy marriage for a very long time. She did the right thing and now it was her turn to live.

I really got a kick out of everything she was doing. She was driving all over the place visiting people and doing things. One day she decided to drive out to New Jersey to visit her cousin. She would be staying there for the weekend. That evening we got a phone call from Harold's brother. Mom was in the hospital. She was experiencing pains in her chest so she went to the emergency room to make sure she was okay. The diagnosis was angina. Harold' brother had driven out to see what was going on. Harold spoke to his brother and said he would drive out first thing in the morning.

Jesse was about 8 months old at the time. We had him on the pillow between us in our bed. I was lying on my stomach and I felt a chill cross over from my right shoulder across my back to the other side. It was enough of a chill to make me open my eyes to see what it was. I was facing Jesse at the time. As my baby boy slept he put a big smile on his face. I instinctively knew what happened.

I started to shake my husband. After a few minutes he woke up and asked me why I woke him. I told him that I just felt his mother cross over my back to get to her grandson. She had kissed him goodbye. He looked at me like I was crazy and said she was fine. I insisted that something was wrong. We received the phone call within fifteen minutes. Mom had passed away in the hospital of a heart attack. Harold was distraught that he never got to see his mother in the physical plane before she passed over.

My husband was always a skeptic. Over the years after seeing more and more happen he has finally come around. Although still skeptical about a few things, he has opened his mind to a lot. He has learned that when I say something he should probably listen!

Chapter Twenty Three

"Chicken Pox"

Jesse came home from kindergarten. He looked like he was a little bit under the weather but he wasn't complaining of anything and he was pretty much acting like his usual self. It was a few days before Halloween. That evening I noticed that he had a few little pimples that were coming out on his abdomen. I called the school and sure enough a few children had come down with chicken pox.

Other than having a handful of pox and running a very low grade fever the kid was okay. Three days later I dressed him up as a cowboy and off we went to trick or treat. I was hoping that Kali would catch them from him and get it over with. That's how we used to do it back then. Parents would actually bring their children around kids that had the chicken pox so they would contract them. It's one of those diseases they say you only get once.

I was not concerned with myself because I was sure I had them. I actually helped out my sister and took care of her girls' years earlier when she had contracted them. I figured if I didn't get them then, I must have had them previously. I was a sickly child so I assumed I had most everything. I remember having pneumonia, bronchitis and always convulsing. Unfortunately, any records kept by my mother were long gone.

One evening exactly ten days after Jesse's break out, I was lying in bed and my belly was itching. I scratched it not thinking it was anything out of the norm. No matter how much I scratched I couldn't stop the itching. I finally got up out of bed and went to the bathroom to see what was going on. I flipped on the light and there they were CHICKEN POX! My stomach was covered with little red pimples and they were driving me insane. I couldn't believe what I was seeing. I did recall feeling a little funny that day but it never dawned on me that I could be getting sick.

Within twenty-four hours I was loaded with pox. I remember how sick I felt. Chicken Pox as an adult can be very dangerous. Not only did I contract them but my daughter Kali did too. She was about 2 years old. I felt so guilty about not being able to help her but honestly I couldn't even move. My husband actually had to take a week off of work to care for us.

One early evening about 3 or 4 days into the illness I was lying in bed so sick I couldn't lift my head from the pillow. I had a very high fever and probably should have been hospitalized. I called the doctor earlier that day and he basically told me if I was able to speak to him that coherently I was handling it very well. It sure didn't feel that way.

As I was lying on my bed with my eyes closed I heard my name being called. I immediately recognized the voice although I hadn't heard it in many years. I opened my eyes and turned my head towards the bedroom door. Standing there with a big smile on his face was my dad.

My father died when I was fourteen and we all missed him so much. My sister, brother and I all had an incredible relationship with him. My brother was only four years old when my dad passed away and to this day at age forty-one he still holds the wonderful memories close to his heart. That goes to show you what an impact love makes, especially a fathers' love for his children.

I never really dreamt of my father since his death. I think deep down inside I was so angry at him for leaving us. I know he had no control over that but I assumed since our mother was taken so young he'd be around forever. The few times I did dream of him I had a feeling of being abandoned. He was standing there clear as day. I looked at him and I said, "Dad, I miss you so much. What are you doing here?" He started to speak to me. His conversation was about his grandchildren and how he was always watching us. He spoke about my sister, brother and I. and all his grandchildren as his face was beaming with love and pride. He told me that he is always around all three of us and will continue to watch.

I just sat and listened in awe. I remember feeling so happy. Finally he said, "I have to go sweetheart." I turned onto my side and reached for him. He backed away and said, "You cannot touch me honey." I responded, "But Dad I want to hug you. Don't leave me. I want to go with you!" He looked at me and said, "Honey, you cannot come with me. You still have things to do here. You will see me again someday but not for a very long time. You keep doing what you're doing and take care of my beautiful grandchildren. I love you." As quickly as he came he was gone.

My husband heard me mumbling from the other room and came in to see who I was talking to. I told him I was talking to my father. He looked at me and said," Jan you're father has been gone for twenty years."

As the days went by I started feeling better. I was talking to someone on the phone and mentioned what had happened. I told her about seeing my father and mentioned I was hallucinating from the fever. She said, " Jan, you weren't hallucinating. He was with you." The more I thought about it the more it made sense. I really should have been in the hospital. My fever was extremely high. I felt like I was knocking at deaths door.

The veil between the living and the dead grows very thin when you are very ill. I do believe that really was my dad beside me. I do know he wanted to deliver those messages. Although nothing he said was life changing it was reassuring to know he's been there all along. It's also nice to know I'll be around to accomplish what I'd like to!

Chapter Twenty Four

"Grandpa Watching"

There are some things that I was told by my Grandma Di that I will never forget. One bit of information was about my home. My grandfather died at a pretty young age. It was winter and he was shoveling snow in the driveway. My grandma went outside to check on him because she didn't hear him out there. When she got outside she saw him lying in the snow. He had a massive heart attack.

I believe it was in the early 50's that he passed. Now according to her they actually waked my grandfather in the house I live in. Apparently this was a common practice back then. I remember I used to think that I was sleeping in the same exact spot the coffin was. I always took comfort and still do that his spirit still pops in every now and then.

Occasionally I will see an apparition just standing in the hallway. After a few minutes it will just drop through the floor quickly. It's always in the same spot in the hall and I feel it's my grandpa just checking things out. It's actually really nice to have family members around.

I am not the only one who has seen him. I remember the day my son Jesse mentioned the man in the hallway. He always stands in the same spot. It's just inside the second door. Now where he was laid out is just on the other side of the wall. It's almost like he stands there showing us he is still protecting his home and family. That's what I like to believe anyway.

Chapter Twenty Five
"The Man in the Mirror"

It was about eleven years ago that my sister Dee and my nephew Dom moved into the apartment downstairs. It was a really good time for all of us. It was another step in her independence from a failed marriage and I got my sister in the same home as me!

Moving in was easy. She really didn't bring much with her only the necessities. Her bedroom furniture, personal stuff, clothes etc. Dom ended up taking his sister Jaime's bedroom set. The set was black lacquer with a very large mirror that attached to the back of the headboard.

The bed in Dom's room was set up so that the mirror was facing the bedroom door. Off of his bedroom is the living room which has a doorway to the hall. Off of the hallway is the bathroom.

A couple of years passed and all was calm. They were settled in very comfortably in their place. I don't know exactly what time in the early morning it was but Dom got up to use the bathroom. After he was done, he walked slowly back to his room.

As he was walking through the living room he happened to look up into the mirror behind his bed. There in the mirror right behind him was the figure of a man slowly moving towards him. Dom ran, slammed the door, jumped into bed and pulled the covers up over his head. I will never forget the look on his face when he was telling me the story the following day. He was coming to me for answers and this time I had one!

The more Dom described the man he saw the more it dawned on me who it was. When I was a child my great-grandpa Siino used to live with us. His bedroom was down stairs off the same hall the bathroom was located. I remember going into his room when I was young and holding his hand. He actually died in that room. I don't know what year it was but I was still a small child. It was like one day he was there and the next he was gone. I know in my heart that the apparition Dom saw was grandpa Siino. I told Dom not to sweat it that it was his great-great grandfather. He said he was fine with that but he just didn't want to be startled again. I told him to go downstairs and tell grandpa that. I don't think he ever saw him again!

Chapter Twenty Six
"The Man in the Hospital Gown"

The only time I know of that my niece Jaime saw anything was about six years ago. At the time she was living down the Bronx on Rhinelander Avenue. That street is basically a couple of blocks away from a few medical centers, Jacobi, Einstein and Montefiore. It is very high energy (as is with all hospital areas).

She was a passenger in her boyfriend's car. They were stopped at a red light right beside one of the hospitals. It was evening. Jaime turned to glance out the window and when she did she jumped out of her seat. There standing right outside the car looking in the window was an old man in a hospital gown.

When she called me to tell me she said the figure was so solid she thought this man had walked out of the hospital. When she took a second look he was gone. Not only gone but nowhere in sight. It was then that it dawned on her she had seen a ghost. She saw a full bodied solid apparition. She hit the jackpot with her first experience. I told her not to be surprised if she saw things again. This may just be the beginning!

Chapter Twenty Seven
"The Soldier"

It was quite a few summers ago that my husband Harold had his first encounter with an apparition. It was a really hot summer night. He was out in the garage like he often is working on one of his projects. On this particular evening, he had the garage doors open. It was balmy out because it was so hot and it was drizzling on and off all evening. There was a light fog that had settled in the yard. He wanted to get the project done so it was going into the early hours of the morning. It was about one a.m. or so.

I was upstairs sleeping when he came in. He woke me up to tell me about what he saw. He wasn't frightened but he was extremely excited. He said he had his head under the hood of the car he was working on. He happened to glance up and to his surprise, there floating across the yard very slowly was a confederate soldier. He said he saw it very distinctly. He saw the uniform, hat and firearm at his side. He stood there in awe and didn't move until it had passed right through the fence.

I really wasn't surprised that he saw this. Sometimes when you live in a place all your life you forget about its history. We live in an area that is off of one of the original roads that led from the North to the South called Boston Post Road. The area where our house is built could very well have been an area where troops would have camped out for the night. A bit into the woods but not too far off the main road. That was the only time my husband ever saw a spirit. That encounter was enough to turn him into a believer!

Chapter Twenty Eight

"The Man with the Cigar"

Harold and I were married for about 7 years when Grandma Di Passed away. Two years later we decided to buy her house. There was plenty of work that needed to be done in this house basically being ignored for years. Harold and I did whatever we could with the little amount of money we saved. This house took everything we had.

We managed to scrape up a bit to do some renovation. Jesse and Kali had been sharing a room and we decided that we needed to separate them. At that point we changed our dining room into a third bedroom for our son.

My home has always been owned by family. Many years earlier my Uncle Jack and Aunt Laura lived in my apartment upstairs. It is where my family and I live now. My father and Aunt Laura were very good friends. He would come upstairs often and hang out in the dining room. Aunt Laura said he sat in the same chair all the time.

One day after Jesse had been sleeping in his room for about a month he started talking about the man that came into his room at night. Knowing that he could very well be sensitive I started to question him a bit more. Jesse told me that he liked the man that came to him. He said the man joked with him all the time and he was always smiling and laughing.

I assumed that he had made contact with a spirit. What spirit I didn't know. Jesse went on to describe that the man wore a white shirt with no sleeves and he wore green pants. I never thought anything of it because I figured as long as he wasn't afraid of the man I had no problem with it. Jesse would tell me different things the man had said to him. One of the things Jesse said the man told him was, "I am your angel. I am always watching you."

Time passed and my son would tell me about other things the angel said. Finally he said, "Mommy, I just don't like the smoke. "I asked him," What smoke honey?" He said," The man smokes something and I don't like the smell."

Now both my parents died very young and had been gone for quite a long time. One day I decided to show my son some old pictures. I showed him his grandpa and grandma on his Daddy's side and then I showed him my parents. He started pointing frantically. "Mommy ,Mommy that's the man. That's my Angel!" Sure enough it was my father.

All at once all the pieces to the puzzle fell into place. The white tee shirt and green pants. Those were his work clothes. He always wore white tees and dark green workpants. My father was also an avid cigar smoker. I remember how we would find cigar ashes here and there on the floor. He always walked around with a cigar in his mouth. That's what my son was talking about when he said he didn't like the smoke. He was smelling cigar smoke.

Obviously my father was the one who was coming to my son at night. It also made sense that Jesse's bedroom was the old dining room where my father always sat when he visited upstairs. My father had come through once again. He really is always watching. Although I knew he was "sensitive" that was the first time I realized my son was just like me.

Chapter Twenty Nine

"I Am Here To Catch You"

There was a period about twelve years ago that changed my sister Dee's life. She was married very young. I think she was nineteen. She ended up marrying a high school sweetheart and never imagined that it would end the way it did. Not only was she lied to and deceived by her ex -husband she was also betrayed by her friend. Remember the big Karmic no-no's. Well this fit into one of those categories.

My sister was married twenty three years and raised four great children. Before the truth was revealed there was quite a bit of back and forth on her ex's part. She had no idea that he had been cheating on her all along and assumed that he was going through some type of mid-life crisis. She called me one afternoon to tell about something odd that happened to her.

She told me that she was standing in the kitchen sorting through the mail and suddenly felt a pair of arms surround her. She said it felt so real that she actually turned around thinking one of her daughters had come up behind her. When she turned no one was there.

At that time she also said that she just felt the presence of my father around her all day. It wasn't near his birthday or any anniversaries so we couldn't really figure out what was bringing him around. A few days later everything came to a head. The truth was revealed as to what was really going on. She found out that her ex had been cheating and who he was cheating with.

Now my father's presence was starting to make sense. We both believe his spirit was there trying to warn and comfort her as to what was coming. It was my father's way of being there for her. Even though it was very hard for her at the time, the fact that she knew my dad was there was a big help to her. His presence gave her faith that she would make it through this crisis.

I am glad to say she is happier than she has ever been in her life. This whole event ended up being the best thing that could ever happen to her. She has a good honest man in her life and is surrounded by her beautiful children and grandchildren! My sister is being rewarded for all the good things she does in her life. That is the perfect example of good karma!

My main guide. My mother Marisa (Marie)

My father Sam. He comes around in times of need.

"Paris"our chihuahua. She was a gift from St. Francis.

A picture of our hallway. This is where the image of my
grandfather appears briefly before dropping through the floor.

Our miracle twins. They have already shown a connection to the other side. They started communicating with "Marie" by age 4.

Our beautiful Sammi. She turned one of our darkest days light again. She is also the namesake to her grandpa Sam.

My mother-in-law Nicky. She came to me in a dream
to deliver a message to her daughter Joann.

An amazing psychic and sister witch Kelly Curtis Spangler
and I. This picture was taken when we attended the
"Witches Ball" in Salem, Massachusetts.

My gorgeous daughter Kali. She has an unusual
knack for communicating with animals.

My son Jesse. He started communicating with the "Man with the
Cigar" at age 6. His sensitivities became apparent at a very early age.

My husband Harold at the Willows in Salem, Mass.
He was a skeptic until experiencing a specter from
the Civil War walking across our backyard.

One of my watercolors inspired by the "Old Burying
Point" in my beloved Salem, Massachusetts.

Part Three

"On To the Next Generation"

Chapter Thirty

"The Twins........Our Miracles"

I am so blessed to be able to actually sit here and write about my great nieces Gia Marie and Ava Marisa. They were born extremely premature and we had no idea if they would survive or if there would be any complications. Eight years later they are thriving and absolutely beautiful. I know not everyone believes in miracles but they do exist. Everyone in my family will attest to that.

"TWINS"

My niece had been trying to get pregnant for a little over a year. She could not conceive. It came time to make a decision. Her husband and she decided to go with In Vitro. It was a very tense time for her but she wanted nothing more than to be a mother. I remember telling her I had a feeling she would carry twins. Not only because of the In Vitro but because twins run in our family.

She was praying to only have to go through the procedure once. She actually signed a release form for the specialist to implant an extra egg during the procedure. Time passed and our prayers were answered. Janine was pregnant!

They had come by my sisters' house to give her the good news. My niece turned around and said, "I hate to disappoint you Aunt Jan but only one egg attached. I am not having twins. "They had gone to the doctor earlier that day. She was healthy. The egg implanted itself, single birth according to the doctor. I never go back on what I say when I feel something in my gut. I said," I am thrilled for you two but I still say you're having twins. "They both kind of looked at me and we moved on to chat about other things.

Two weeks later I got a phone call. It was my niece Janine. I could hear the excitement in her voice. She had gone to see her doctor for her weekly checkup. "Aunt Jan I have some news! I'm having twins!" Ahhhhhh....I knew it! She was laughing on the phone and wanted to tell me first. "You were right again." Apparently the egg that did implant was a twin egg that split. The girls are identical (mirror) twins. That was the beginning of our beautiful girls' journey.

Chapter Thirty One
"Angel in the Elevator"

It was May 21st. We never expected to hear Janine was in labor. Normally we would have been thrilled but it was too soon. The girls weren't due until August. Janine was going to the hospital. My sister ran there and shortly after I followed. One of the twins was leaning on the mother's cervix which had started the contractions. While we were there they had given Janine a medication to stop them. Things were calming down until she suddenly started to develop pneumonia. Apparently this is something that can happen on this particular medication.

My niece had nurses checking on her constantly. Being that we were staying with her we had seen quite a few come and go. They were changing shifts every few hours. As the hours progressed, Janine was getting worse. Ultimately they were going to transport her down to Columbia Presbyterian hospital. They have an amazing Neonatal wing there. It looked like these babies were going to be born.

I decided to go home for a while. There was nothing we could do while she was being transported down there. I said my goodbyes and got into the elevator. Just before the doors closed a woman dressed in scrubs got in. I asked her what floor she wanted pushed the button and the doors closed.

I looked at the woman whom I'm assuming was a nurse and tried to figure out if I had seen her on the maternity floor. I never saw her before. Out of nowhere she turned to me and said," He hears you, you know." I said, "Excuse me? Who hears me?" She lifted her eyes up pointed upward and said, "He's hearing your prayers."

The elevator stopped and off she went. I dropped my keys on the floor. I picked them up quickly, looked up and she was gone. I looked to the right and the left. SHE WAS NOWHERE TO BE FOUND ! There is no way she could have gotten across the lobby that quickly. It was then that I realized I was in the elevator with a messenger. Once again an angel appeared to me, this time in a human form.

As I stated before the girls are beautiful and thriving. Not only are they thriving but there are no complications whatsoever from their premature births. I also think that it's kind of cool that they were born on the cusp. The cusp of Taurus the bull and you guessed it Gemini the twins!

Chapter Thirty Two
"Gia and Ava's Imaginary Friend"

I always felt he" gift" gets passed down through family members and generations. From what I have read about twins there seems to be a natural ability towards having a sixth sense. The bond between twins is strong and seems to never break. If you would see these sisters together your heart would melt. They truly are like two peas in a pod.

The girls shared a bedroom and when they were about four my niece noticed signs of them having an imaginary friend. It was the usual stuff. They would sit playing games, giggling looking at books. My niece never thought anything about it and it continued on for a while.

One day my niece decided to ask the girls a few questions. She was asking about their friend and to her surprise the person they described was an older woman. The girls kept saying she was like a grandma. Janine finally asked," What is your friend's Name?" The response was "Marisa."

My niece nearly fell off her chair. The person they were talking to was their great-grandmother. The reason why she knew this was because of the name. Marisa (pronounced Mareesa) is not a very common name here in the states. My mother was definitely in Janine's house communicating with the girls.

As Janine thought about it there were a few little things that were happening that were odd. One incident that kept happening was she kept finding the spoon rest on her stove moved. When I went to her house one of the things I mentioned to her was the strong presence I felt in the kitchen. You could feel my Mom hanging around the stove. That just confirmed what Janine was finding.

Janine also mentioned that a photo she had of my mother on her television had fallen over the previous week. That was definitely my mother letting her granddaughter know she was there. I believe that until this day the girls will mention their friend now and then. This only proves what I know to be true. They are both naturally gifted!

Chapter Thirty Three
"Our Beautiful Sammi"

Ten months after the twins were born, our family got even more wonderful news. My niece Janine announced that she was pregnant! We were all thrilled to death. I was speaking to my niece and she had said that if she had a boy she would name him Sam after my dad and if it was another girl, she would be Samantha. Either way this child would be named after my father. She was going to call the baby Sammi.

Her official due date was December 8th and we were all anxiously awaiting the birth of Sammi. At that time, I was running a lunch program at the school my children attended. My partner and I were taking night classes at Westchester Community College so we could get certified in food service.

Our courses were every Wednesday night for eight weeks. One night in November after class, I saw that my phone had a message on it. When I retrieved the message it said that Janine had the baby. I couldn't believe she was early again. I called my sister to get the details and sure enough Sammi had arrived.

While I was speaking to my sister she said, "You know what day it is right?" Yes, I did. It was the anniversary of the day my father died, November 16th.For years I had dreaded this day. It was a very painful memory.

I asked my sister what time the baby had arrived. She said 6:34 p.m. I remembered my father had passed away sometime around dinner. I had my father's death certificate and was determined to check out the Time of Death.

I rushed home and went immediately into my lockbox. There in the envelope was the death certificate. T.O.D.(time of death) 6:34 p.m. I immediately called my sister and told her what I had found. She was as shocked as I was. Not only was she named after him, she was born on the day of his death at the exact time of his death.

Now I know there are a lot of non- believers out there but I do not believe in coincidence. Even if I did this was a little too much. Like my sister Dee said, after all these years of sadness on this date, Daddy finally gave us something to be happy about. From now on we will be celebrating our Sammi's birthday!

Part Four

"Animals and Demons"

Chapter Thirty Four
"Kali of the Animal Kingdom"

My daughter Kali has always been an avid animal lover. Not only does she love animals but any living thing. She was the child that used to bring me cicada bug shells and" rolly" bugs from underneath rocks. It was pretty funny actually. She was always 100% girl right down to refusing to wear pants because "she was a girl!" She rolled over rocks, dug in the dirt and was always saving strays. There was nothing cuter than seeing her march outdoors on a summer night in her little cotton dress with a flashlight in her hand.

Kali's abilities lie with communicating with animals either dead or living. She has an uncanny sense to communicate with any animal which prompted one of her nicknames "Dr. Doolittle."

When she was about six years old she was begging me for a bird. Our neighbor had a cockatoo and she would go over there almost daily to play with him. I respect all living things but quite honestly I am not really a bird person. The begging and carrying on to purchase a bird was going on for weeks. Finally one afternoon my sister and I were sitting in the yard. Kali was whining about the bird. In comes Aunt Dee Dee with her solution to the problem.

She pulled Kali aside and told her that if she prayed to God hard enough he would send her a bird. I thought that was genius! Kali was satisfied with that and that evening I found her on her knees by her bed praying for her bird. It was such a sweet sight.

Two or three days later, Kali came running upstairs extremely excited. "Mommy, Mommy, GOD SENT ME A BIRD! "I said, "What? "She replied "God sent me a bird. He is white. He flew into the driveway and he followed me Mommy. He loves me. It's my bird. God heard my prayers!"

I couldn't comprehend what this child was saying. I followed her down the stairs and sure enough waiting there at the top of the driveway was a white carrier pigeon. Kali ran down the steps and said "See mommy. It's my bird, watch." I watched as she started to walk back down the driveway. Off she walked in her little jellies closely followed by her new feathered friend. She commanded follow and so it did.

This went on for a good five hours or so. In the meantime I was on the phone with Aunt Dee telling her what was going on. She thought it was hilarious, I wanted to kick her butt ! The bird finally took off. I really thought she was going to be crushed but thankfully she had enough of the bird for one day and she was convinced it would return.

We never did see that bird again but this is just one of many of the incidents that occurred with Kali's communication with animals. I know it seems crazy but I swear that bird understood everything she said.

Kali doesn't really talk about anything that she sees but I will tell you this, from the moment I looked into that kid's eyes I knew she was an old soul. She has never given me one day of grief and is one of the wisest people I know. Although she is just twenty years old I go to her for advice. When Kali speaks......Mommy listens!

Chapter Thirty Five

"Rain" (A Beloved Pet)

I am a very lucky woman in how I get to meet a lot of really wonderful people in my line of work. One of these people is Katherine. I met Katherine about a year ago through someone I knew. I think there is a reason to meet everyone you do. Somewhere along the line you usually see the purpose. Katherine and I immediately became friends. She also happens to be a witch. That is always a plus!

I liked and admired her from the first time I met her. Katherine is the maker of magical things. She hand crafts staffs, jewelry, wands and more. Everything she creates has her own magic in it. All of it is absolutely beautiful. She is also a practicing witch and lives her life "clean." She is a good woman with good Karma who is proving to be a good friend. As I got to know her I learned about her beloved German Shepherd Rain. There were photos of Rain in her home. You could tell how much she loved that dog.

One day we were talking on the phone. As we were chatting away I distinctly heard the bark of a dog. It was not only the bark of a dog but the bark of a German Shepherd. I know the bark well because my neighbor has the same breed of dog. After I heard it I asked her if she had heard it too. She said no she didn't. She asked me what it meant and I told her that it was Rain's way of telling her she was around her and that she loved her. Our conversation ended and we left it at that.

A few days later I got a phone call from a mutual acquaintance. She told me that Katherine had called her and was very excited. She said she had been cleaning and stuck her hand behind one of the cushions of her couch. To her surprise tucked behind the cushion was one of Rain's bones! That was the validation that her pet was still around her. That was the sign. Unconditional love in life and death!

Chapter Thirty Six

"A Gift From St. Francis"

Here and there when my children were growing up I would hear that common question. The question was " Mom, can we get a dog? " I am an animal lover specifically when it comes to dogs. The best present I ever got was on my eighth birthday. I was in the basement with all my friends having a party. My dad walked in and said," Happy Birthday! "I remember being excited to see him. I adored my dad but I was also a little disappointed that I didn't see a present in his hands.

I went to hug him and I saw the pocket on his jacket move. I jumped back a little scared and let out a squeal. My dad stuck his hand in his jacket pocket and pulled out the most precious ball of white fur I ever saw in my life. It was a miniature toy poodle, Misty. I went nuts! I adored that little puppy and would play with her for hours. As time went on she ended up with my Grandma Di. You know how that goes. Once we get a taste of hanging out with our friends we are too busy to take care of a pet.

When Misty was finally put to sleep I was sick. My heart was breaking and I remember crying for days. That is the exact reason why I always avoided the question from my kids. It's not because I didn't want them to have a dog, it was because I didn't want them to go through the sense of loss when the animal passes. I remember how hard they cried when Flounder and Sebastian died and they were goldfish.

It was the summer of 2004 and at that time a lot of changes were occurring in my life. My husband and I were constantly bickering and it was a really rough year for me. A lot of the arguing had to do with him being out of work. If anything makes a couple fight it is money. I was so depressed and things were continuing to get tighter financially.

I always told my children that the only way I would get a dog is through a miracle. It would literally have to fall in to my lap. Enter my friend Donna.

Donna is the earthbound St. Francis. This woman is constantly rescuing stray animals from all over the place. Although she wouldn't admit it she has a big heart and is one of the best friends anyone can ever have. I am blessed to have her in my life. She's also one of the craziest people I know. I mean that kind of crazy that is good!

One afternoon I got a call from Donna. She said she was stopping by to show me her new dog. She made me laugh because she didn't tell her husband about her yet. She already has a sweet pit bull named Godiva.

In she came with her new dog. I was sitting at the dining room table. Donna walked over and placed the most precious little dog in my lap. It was a Chihuahua. Tan and white deer head Chihuahua. I know we moms are partial to our children but my Paris is absolutely adorable (yes I consider her one of my kids). She looked up at me and it was all over. I fell in love on the spot. She has been with us ever since.

I prayed to all the saints during that dark period in my marriage. I know in my heart one of the saints that heard me was St. Francis. I believe he brought this precious animal in my life to make me smile and give me some happiness. I have been smiling for nine years now. Paris is my best friend and yes as far as I am concerned, a miracle.

Chapter Thirty Seven

"Was That An Incubus?"

It was about fifteen years ago. If I remember correctly it was about 5:30 A.M. My husband was sound asleep right next to me. I had woken up (one of many times during the night) and was having a hard time getting back to sleep. I felt very uneasy and had an overwhelming feeling of being watched. I had a strange sense of something being in my room at the foot of my bed. I pulled myself up on my elbows and glanced down towards my feet. I saw nothing. I laid back down and tried settling in when I felt a tug on my blanket. I slid my feet up and glanced at the foot of the bed once more. This time I could have sworn I saw something looking back. It was black with reddish eyes and it was peeking over the foot of the bed at me.

I knew something wasn't right as soon as I felt the pressure at the bottom of my bed. Something was coming towards me and I felt absolutely helpless. I was terrified to look at it because the glance I did get was horrid. Black and shiny with tiny slanted eyes.

I instinctively started to chant to protect myself and demand that it leave. I really believe this "thing" didn't expect me to challenge it and when I began to chant and pray I threw it off guard for a split second. That was the moment I reacted.

I sprang out of my bed and smacked the light switch on. There on my wall was what looked like an oil spot with eyes. Its body was shiny and in constant motion. It was slithering from my ceiling upside down towards my window. It lifted its head for a brief moment. It was hideous. It looked at me and snarled. As soon as it made it to my window it exited very quickly. It was almost as if it was sucked into the dawn.

I always thought it was some kind of a night terror but years later I realized that "thing" was probably an Incubus. All I can say is I will never forget what this "thing" looked like and I pray I never see it again.

Chapter Thirty Eight
"The Lioness"

I have to say that I have been very lucky to have had the mother I did. Although it was for a very short time, she was the one who passed her gifts down to me. She made me understand what was happening and taught me to never be afraid. I always felt my gifts were normal. I had an amazing childhood and she is still with me to this day. As fiercely as a lioness protects her cubs my mother stands before me.

There have been a few times that I have run into some not so nice entities. I recall one particular time I was being circled by a disturbed, vicious demon like being. This being was dark not only in spirit but literally. A little grey creature that leered at me and was trying it's hardest to intimidate me. I was using the Ovilus[*] at the time and I remember saying," I don't fear you because I am protected. I walk in the light and am surrounded by love, purity and my guides." At that moment the Ovilus said one word," Marisa !" I knew exactly what it meant. Marisa was protecting her cub with a vengeance. Don't get me wrong, I'm not an idiot. I don't ever go looking for these things but in the event one happens to mess with me, I know my mother is standing fiercely in front of me.

---

[*] Ovilus – an electronic speech- synthesis device which delivers words depending on environmental readings including electromagnetic waves.

Part Five

"And In the End......."

Chapter Thirty Nine

"Spirit Guides"

The Fabulous Four

Everyone has spirit guides. These are the guides that help bring information or other spirit through to you. To date, I have connected to four spirit guides. They tend to come into your life at any random time. I feel the guides I have all represent different aspects in my life. Once a guide comes into your life, they are there for the long haul. A guide can be a deceased relative, a child, a spiritual leader. There is really no limitation on time. It's just like the Universe. The following is a few words on the guides that have chosen me.

Marisa (Marie, my Mother)

Standing in the forefront protecting me and running the show is my mother. As I pointed out earlier I have always had a very deep connection with her. As a child I remember communicating with her through thoughts. Funny, it was almost like she was preparing me on how to open the channel. This is how I get most of my messages through images and thoughts. Mom is with me twenty four hours a day, seven days a week, every waking and sleeping moment of my life! I take such comfort in knowing she is always with me. I have been told by three prominent people in the paranormal field that she is always present.

It doesn't surprise me how she protects both me and my sister. How we are in life is how we are in death. She has passed the gift to both my sister and I. The only difference is I have chosen to use mine more. It has been present for generations on my mom's side of the family. I have now passed it on to both of my children and my sister has done the same. Marie is always here protecting my space.

I have actually felt spirit draw back if it was someone who had too much heavy energy or would have drained me too much. It saves me from having to push away myself. Marie's presence is very strong. She is my protector.

Naraju (The Babylonian Warrior)

I came upon Naraju during a ritual which involved regressing into the past. I was in Salem, Massachusetts performing a ritual for Lughnassad. The ritual was being led by an amazing witch and friend Kelly Spangler. She took us back and we were in a field of wheat speaking to our clan leader.

I saw Kelly and myself very distinctively and was communicating with her. I remember speaking about the harvest and how it was too hot that summer. I remember seeing fires in the distance and I could even smell the crops burning. In my regression we were performing a ritual for rain to help the crops, a ritual within a ritual...very cool.

I was a male. I was a warrior. Upon my head were Ram horns and I was wearing deer skin pants. I also had a breastplate made of bones. I was speaking to Kelly in a foreign tongue and she was replying. I understood every word she said and even called her by a name, Inana.

When we finally came back to the present we found we realized we were speaking in an ancient language. We were in sync with our movements. When we researched what we had said and how we were dressed it was in front of our eyes. The warrior with the horns and the breastplate and the goddess with the headpiece made of wheat. The language we were speaking was ancient Sumerian. I instinctively knew my name was Naraju.

My warrior has been with me ever since. He stands alongside my mother ready for battle. I often call on him during my spell work. Once while I was casting I saw the face of a wolf in the candle holder. The wolf is the spirit of this warrior. Power, cunning, strength and courage are what Naraju brings with him.

The Little Girl

Now as you may notice, there is no name for this guide. She keeps changing it! She once told me her name was Angelique, another time Britt. I think she just likes to play make believe. For this story I will refer to her as Angel. Angel found me on an investigation about ten years ago. My friend Jean who had 3 boys at the time was living in a very old building one town over. As time passed she was experiencing different things in her place and they were getting more frequent.

It started off with little things like missing keys, finding dishes stacked on her kitchen floor etc. At first it was no big deal but eventually someone was relighting a candle. That was a problem. That needed to be addressed. No one should live in fear of a fire starting.

Another re-occurring incident was she would constantly find the throw rug in her sons' room (the rug was shaped like a rocket) pointing towards a particular corner. When her son started communicating with his "friend" she needed to get answers and asked me if I could come by to see what was happening.

I walked into the apartment and immediately saw Angel run from the hallway into the boys' room. The closet door was moving and there huddled in the corner she sat, peeking up at me from behind her crossed arms. I looked at her and told her not to be afraid. I wasn't there to hurt her. I wanted to help her. I asked her to please show me something about herself. The room immediately changed. It was pink with floral wallpaper, and the furniture was rearranged. There was a bed that was in the corner. She was pointing the rug towards the bed. That's where it was during her life. Now things were making sense.

She told me she missed her mommy and loved to watch my friend spending time with her kids. All she wanted was a Mom figure and some attention. I told her I would be her mother figure if she liked. She ran from the closet and hugged my friend and I at the same time. We both felt the cold on our legs. The feeling was so overwhelming we both sobbed.

Angel has been with me ever since that day. She is a playful loving little girl who loves to be mischievous. She plays with your hair, giggles, hide your keys. She is youth and is my child guide.

Matthew (The Young Man)

Matthew is my newest addition. He has recently introduced himself to me. I attended a workshop in May of 2012 that connected us to our higher spiritual self. It was a wonderful program that helped me to re connect. Each participant was led into the center of the room and was placed into the column of light. The column of light is an energy force that is being generated by a circle of people around you. It is truly amazing the power and vibration that is felt. I was led into the center and my chakras were cleared. I was told to continue using my gift and that I was given more.

I went to sleep and at about 2 A.M. I opened my eyes peacefully.

I woke because I could feel someone near me. There he was kneeling beside my bed. He was a young man wearing jeans and a button down plaid shirt. He looked exactly like Matthew McConaughey. That's where the name came from. I smiled at him, he smiled back and I instinctively knew he was my newest guide.

Matthew reminds me to not be so hard on myself. He brings me Peace and is my nature guide.

Chapter Forty

"Religion and the Craft"

Unfortunately there are many pre conceived opinions about witchcraft. I myself battled with it for a very long time. I knew what I was feeling. I knew what I was manifesting. I instinctively knew what to use at different times for different situations. When I discussed this with my mentor Lori Bruno she stated,"Janny, you aren't learning you are remembering!" With that remembrance always came this underlying guilt that what I was believing and manifesting was wrong.

Is it wrong to believe there might be more out there? I have a very strong belief in God. I just feel that organized religions have limited our potential. There have been too many men attaching too many rules and regulations to something that should be pure and from the heart.

I never slam anyone's beliefs. To each his own. I just reserve the right to have the same courtesy extended and think there is more to it. It took me a very long time to find the right fit. I was so bogged down with guilt and conditioning that I was my own worst enemy. I never understood if we were Christians who were supposed to live our lives in the light of God, why didn't we have tolerance and understanding. Doesn't God love everyone? Why would anyone be judged for not fitting into the mold? Our differences are what make us all beautiful.

Every time I went to confession I never understood why I had to sit in a dark room and talk to a priest about what I did wrong? What sins could I have possibly committed at the age of 7? Don't misunderstand I am happy to have a strong religious background. The good absolutely outweighs the bad but again life isn't so black and white. There's plenty of grey in between, especially in organized religions.

Due to my lack of attendance to church I have heard remarks like, "If you go to church Sunday the pillars will crumble." Um yes whatever. I have grown up around some people who are heartless and cruel. They should never be amongst society. I'm not even going to get into it but they are the first ones in attendance at church on the holidays.

Regardless of what you believe in or who you pray to shouldn't we all have the same goal? Aren't we all here to learn and help one another? Isn't that what it's all about? I believe if you need God (or whoever it is you pray to/worship) God will be there. You don't need to be in a temple or a church. God will hear you wherever you are and help you with whatever you need help with. God or whatever higher power is out there wants us to be happy.

There is the whole ten commandment issue. Honestly other than a guide for being a moral person most of us have broken a few of them. I believe if I am the best person I can be and I help others to the best of my abilities then I am on the right path.

There is so much false information about the craft in the media. No wonder why we are conditioned to view it as a dark or evil thing. First of all there is good and bad in everything. As I read and became more aware of what the truth is I am appalled at what a bad rap the craft gets.

There is a preconception that everyone who is a witch or warlock is Wiccan, absolutely false. There's nothing wrong with being Wiccan just like there's nothing wrong with being any other religion. There are Catholic witches, Jewish witches etc. The Craft is just that. It is a craft like anything else you choose to do. There is nothing wrong in trying to help yourself or others.

Witches, true witches are the kindest most proud intelligent people I know. We respect Mother Earth, we respect all living things, we respect each other. We are kind to animals the elderly, children and anyone else we have the pleasure of meeting. As Lori Bruno coined years ago Wisdom, Integrity, Truth, Courage, Honour, W.I.T.C.H.

Chapter Forty One

"It's Magick"

If you think about it casting a spell is similar to saying a prayer. It is all tied into will and emotion. There is power in words and there is power in groups. Whether it's a church, temple, or coven it's all based on the same concept. Power in numbers, harness the power.

If someone has really hurt another or has tried to attack someone for no reason I'm all for the score being evened. That is justified. Sometimes Karma needs a little push to get the job done. Balance is the key. Most of the time, if you just wish a person back everything they give out to people.....that does the trick. You are reversing the Karma.

There is the question of the three fold law. Not everyone abides by that rule and I'm one of them. It states whatever you do whether good or bad will come back to you three fold. I lean more towards the justice route. In the long run just know that everything has a cause and effect so keep the balance.

Many years ago a very wise man told me, " What's right ...is right!" I always try to live my life by those words. I don't care what everyone else is doing or what they believe. I do what I know in my heart is the right thing. I have always lived my life that way and I know that wise man was right....that wise man was also my dad.

Chapter Forty Two

"Tarot"

Tarot cards have been around since the mid fifteenth century. It is a form of divination along with many others. Most people will come to a tarot reader because they want advice and suggestions on how to handle situations. Now in my experience, there is good and bad in everything. You have some really incredible card readers out there as well as the ones who are along for the ride. The basis of being a good reader is largely the intuitive part of it. The cards are the cards. It is how they are interpreted that makes all the difference.

I believe that anyone who sits in front of me picks the cards they are meant to pick. I don't think anything is coincidence. There is a message to be sent and if a reader is good you will receive it. Any kind of cards whether they be Angel, Earth, Tarot etc. are just a tool in a reading. What the person is truly reading is you. The same applies for ruins, rocks, shells, bones or anything else.

Many a time I have been confronted with someone who disagrees with everything I say or claims it doesn't click with them. I guarantee you somewhere along the line it will. When I read someone I believe in every word I am saying. There are no mistakes in the cards you pick.

The best readers are "connected." They have the ability to see and hear from beyond. Many times what I tell a client is what is being told to me by my guide and or guides at the time. Sometimes it's just one guide, other times they all give me their input. As I described earlier, it seems whoever is the most compatible to whom I am reading usually shows up. Other times attachments to the person I am reading are there. That happens quite often. It can be a friend or relative that has passed. Being a medium keeps you in tune to everything.

I remember once when I was reading at a neighborhood bar a very well dressed woman in her thirties sat down across the table from me. I remember thinking wow she is overdressed. I looked down to grab my cards and when I looked back up a younger girl was sitting down in the same place. There hovering over her left shoulder was the woman.

I asked the woman sitting in front of me if any females in her family had passed. Her eyes got really big and she said her aunt had passed not long ago. I described her and off we went. I have to say her aunt was thrilled! This particular spirit stood the whole time I read her niece throwing in her two sense. When I finished reading her she got up and aunty trailed right along. They must have had an incredible bond when she was alive. I bet you any amount of money that poor girl is having a lot of activity. I don't believe Aunty is going anywhere soon!

In another account about two years ago I had one of the most disturbing readings ever. A young woman who looked to be about twenty-five or so came in and sat across the table from me. As she was picking the cards I was getting flashes of horrible pictures in my head.

I saw her walking down a street at night. I remember thinking it had just rained because the streets were glistening under the street lights. I could actually hear the sound of her heels clicking as she walked along.

Suddenly out of nowhere I saw a tall black figure jump out and grab her. He pulled back her head by her hair and sliced her throat. After that all I saw was blood.

As you can imagine I was terrified for this girl. I didn't want to scare her but I wanted her to be aware. I read her cards and afterwards struck up a conversation. I asked her if she was involved with anyone. She expressed that she had broken up with her boyfriend recently and he was presently stalking her. She proceeded to tell me that she had tried to work it out with him but he was very angry and was doing nothing to control it. I asked her in confidence if he had ever raised his hands to her. She looked at me with tears in her eyes and said yes he had multiple times. That was the vision I was seeing.

I explained to her that I was in a five year abusive relationship years ago. (That is a story for another time.) I had numerous black eyes and a fractured nose compliments of that animal. When I finally left I ran for my life. I wanted her to understand that men like that are very dangerous. I spoke to her for about an hour and continually told her to never walk alone at night and to be extremely careful.

She asked me what I saw. I didn't get into the horrible details but told her what I did see was not pretty. She thanked me and swore she would be extra careful. I haven't seen her since but I know in my heart from the way she listened that she took heed to my warning.

This leads me to why I don't believe in coincidence. That young girl came to me for a reading that night and she walked away with a warning. What are the odds that I would read someone who went through a similar experience that I did so many years ago? She came to me for a reason. It was to save her life.

Reading Children

Everybody has their own opinion about this. I personally keep away from reading anyone under sixteen. I think that children are very impressionable and they can hang on every word you say. I do not want to be responsible for planting a seed in someone so young. I would never give bad advice to anyone but sometimes young minds interpret things differently than they are meant. I also have a hard time seeing a young one in pain. Nothing breaks my heart more than a child going through abuse or addiction.

If for some reason I have to read a child, I always keep it very general. I will discuss interests, maybe bring up something about a pet or school. I will never get deeply into any one subject. I would rather see the smile on a child's face and the surprise when I talk about something close to their heart. The few readings that I have given to kids have gone very well. I would just prefer not to read in such a generalized way.

Responsibility as a Reader

There is a responsibility a reader has towards his or her client. There are some so- called readers that can give really bad advice. Some I have encountered do this for the drama factor. Many others are unstable and honestly should not be giving advice, others should just be committed.

One of the biggest pet peeves I have is when a reader feels they have the right to play God. By this I mean tell someone when they are going to pass away. A few years ago I worked at an event upstate. I asked someone I knew if she would like to work it with me. We were sitting maybe four feet from each other. I was reading an elderly gentleman and she was reading his wife. Suddenly I saw this woman banging on her chest rocking back and forth. I continued on with my reading. After the event was over I asked the reader why that woman was acting the way she was. She stated that the woman was battling breast cancer and asked her when she was going to die. This reader told her she had a few months and should get her things in order.

All I could think was how dare she say that to a woman who was battling for her life. I didn't care if she asked how long she had. No one on the face of this Earth has the right to tell another human being when they will expire. That does not only apply to psychics, it does to EVERYONE. Even doctors should handle this subject with compassion. Everyone has the right to know if they are going to die but who's to say when?

I do believe there is such a thing as miracles. I also believe if someone is fighting for their life every day and a time gets planted into their head the damage is done. Life is precious and we should be allowed to savor every moment without having to worry about our demise. Encourage do not break down. Use your brain and show RESPONSIBILITY!

Chapter Forty Three
"Spirituality"

Spirituality is spirituality folks. No matter how you look at it. Everyone needs something to believe in. Respect Mother Earth and the elements, be a decent human being willing to help others, protect the innocent (children and animals) and live your life being a positive force. I know that is easier said than done because many people just do not get it. It's very hard being a good person in a cruel world. I'm not saying be a doormat, I'm just saying 'think' before you act and try to overlook what you can. Understand that people have emotions like jealousy and anger. Say what you need to say then rise above and let it go.

I once attended a spiritual workshop with someone who was all aglow with positivity and love while we were in the seminar. The minute we were in front of others I became her target. Intimidation is usually a sign of low self- esteem. If someone is unhappy they will try to pull you down with them. Misery loves company.

One of the things they spoke about in the workshop was how the people that don't deserve to be in your life will drop out. Well I got home on a Monday and by Tuesday night the friendship was over. I've never experienced such rage and anger in anyone ever in my life. It takes a lot of energy to hate. Energy is energy and I used all that rage to my advantage. Ultimately the Universe weeded her out of my life because she would never have been a positive force. It is what it is!

I don't wish anyone bad I just chose to keep my life free of negative people. It really is a sin when you don't have the capability of honestly wishing someone well. Instead of trying to tear someone down, get off the couch and do something for yourself.

I have had such wonderful experiences working in Salem at the psychic fair. The set-up is basically ten different psychics sitting side by side in the same room. That's a lot of ego. I never got myself involved in the whole, "Who's the better psychic game." Truthfully we are all good at what we do which is the reason why we are there. I have no problem giving a client to another reader if I feel they may be more suited to them.

Last year I had a woman ask me if I could see what was going on with her land. Although I'm sure I could have given her a decent reading I wanted her to walk away with all her answers. I actually passed her along to one of my colleagues. He has both Native American and Scottish Highlander in his bloodline. He is also very connected to the Earth. I felt he would be the better choice. Turns out I was right. She walked away very satisfied.

"Living My Life"

As far as my everyday life, I have learned to "take it down a notch" when I need my peace. Anyone who is gifted knows that you can never really completely turn it off. I tried that when I finally brought myself around to going to ground zero. I really wanted to be able to heal a bit. It started from about 6 blocks away from the site. The names started running through my head like a ticker tape. I did what I had to but got in and out as quickly as I could. I kind of walked around going through the motions like a zombie.

Aside from the "messages" I live a very normal happy life. I allow spirit to speak and get the messages delivered to the people that need to hear them. I have learned to control the spirit that wants to come through me. I love what I do and am so content to finally live my life helping others.

There are times when what I do can be very hard. It isn't easy having spirit come through you. Being a trans-medium can be very draining. There have been times when I have experienced the pain and twisting of arthritis in my hands, felt the chest pain of a heart attack and experienced the twisting of scoliosis. It isn't very pleasant but I still feel very blessed to bring comfort to others.

All the doors in my life are continuing to open for me. That is how I know I am finally on the right path. In the last few years I have not only found my purpose I have also found my muse. Painting, creating and writing are my passions and I know my guides and loved ones have focused me to forge forward with all these things. I also know that the people who are supposed to be in my life are and the ones who don't deserve to be have dropped out. I have learned some really hard lessons these last few years but looking back at it I know it is all in my best interest. I have learned to "Never say never" and refuse to let the actions of others change who I am. I am enjoying this crazy ride called life and hope to continue writing and creating for many years to come. I also look forward to continue doing my work connecting with spirit in order to help others.

Everyone continue to be the best "You" that you can be and may blessings fall down on all who deserve the best. To everyone else I pray you find your way and understand that we are all here to help each other! Even a smile can go a very long way.

About the Author

Janny realized that she was gifted at a very early age. Always relying on her abilities she started development of her natural medium skills as a child. She receives her messages from the other side through her spirit guides who speak to her or present symbols for her to interpret.

Janny presently works as a psychic/medium/card reader in the New York area and has built a very solid following over the last 3 years. She has showcased her talents at events such as the "Festival of the Dead" psychic fair in Salem, Mass., "Spirit Quest" presented by Ron Kolek and "Carnevale" at The Villa Barone Hilltop Manor in Mahopac, N.Y. She has been a guest on podcasts Ron Kolek presents "Ghost Chronicles" and "Desperate House Witches" on blogtalk radio.

Janny has also had some success as a freelance artist. She currently displays her work at various events and paints whenever her schedule allows her to. She also enjoys writing poetry and short stories.

Wife and mother to two amazing young adults, she considers herself very blessed. Janny will continue to hone her skills and counsel others with her clear sight, compassion and cutting sense of humor.